T0023826

Quaker Quicks — Do Quakers Pray?

What people are saying about

Quaker Quicks — Do Quakers Pray?

Beautifully sculpted, highly accessible, and so full of wisdom and wonderful quotes, this is a book for anyone interested in the practice of prayer not just Quakers. Reading it can be an immersion into prayer itself.

Ben Pink Dandelion, Programmes leader, research, Woodbrooke

This insightful exploration of contemporary Quakers' relationship to and experience of prayer is enriched by the inclusion of a sampling of prayer practices from many faith or wisdom traditions. The narrative illuminates prayer as an active condition of listening, of sensing the Presence of God, and "a movement of the heart". This brief, beautiful, personal text invites the reader to consider prayer as "relationship with all that is" and as a way of being in the world.

Deborah Shaw, Former Assistant Director of Friends Center, Guilford College, North Carolina; author of *Being Fully Present to God*, SEYM

This book is an encouragement – to reflect on our personal practice (why and how we pray – or don't), and to initiate group discussions of a topic which we seem to find faintly embarrassing.

Jennifer Kavanagh offers a brief overview of prayer in different cultures and traditions but mostly the book is grounded in the perspective and experience of contemporary Quakers. She also looks at the differences and similarities between worship and prayer (and her brilliant, wonderfully inclusive description of what is happening in Quaker meeting for worship is worth the cover price alone). In so many ways this book is an invitation "to pray as we can, not as we can't".

Do Quakers pray? Well, yes we do – [despite a] cautiousness around prayer which this wise, timely (and deceptively slim) volume seeks to address. Written for Quakers, it would definitely be of interest to anyone questioning "who or what we pray to". This is an important book, an intelligent and challenging guide for a questioning age.

Alex Wildwood, Associate tutor, Woodbrooke. Co-author of *Rooted in Christianity, Open to New Light*

A useful handbook for those seeking inner peace in a troubled world.

Terry Waite, CBE

Quaker Quicks — Do Quakers Pray?

Jennifer Kavanagh

CHRISTIAN ALTERNATIVE
BOOKS

Winchester, UK
Washington, USA

JOHN HUNT PUBLISHING

First published by Christian Alternative Books, 2023
Christian Alternative Books is an imprint of John Hunt Publishing Ltd.,
No. 3 East St., Alresford, Hampshire SO24 9EE, UK
office@jhpbooks.com
www.johnhuntpublishing.com
www.christian-alternative.com

For distributor details and how to order please visit the 'Ordering' section on our website.

Text copyright: Jennifer Kavanagh 2022

ISBN: 978 1 80341 400 3
978 1 80341 401 0 (ebook)
Library of Congress Control Number: 2022945818

All rights reserved. Except for brief quotations in critical articles or reviews, no part of this book may be reproduced in any manner without prior written permission from the publishers.

The rights of Jennifer Kavanagh as authors have been asserted in accordance with the Copyright, Designs and Patents Act 1988.

A CIP catalogue record for this book is available from the British Library.

Design: Lapiz Digital Services

UK: Printed and bound by CPI Group (UK) Ltd, Croydon, CR0 4YY
Printed in North America by CPI GPS partners

We operate a distinctive and ethical publishing philosophy in all areas of our business, from our global network of authors to production and worldwide distribution.

Contents

Do Quakers Pray?

By the same author

The Methuen Book of Animal Tales (ed.) 9780416247602
The Methuen Book of Humorous Stories (ed.) 9780416506105
Call of the Bell Bird 9780852453650
The World Is Our Cloister 9781846940491
New Light (ed.) 9781846941436
Journey Home (formerly The O of Home) 9781780991511
Simplicity Made Easy 9781846945434
Small Change, Big Deal 9781780993133
The Failure of Success 9789781780998
A Little Book of Unknowing 9781782798088
Heart of Oneness 9781785356858
Practical Mystics 9781789042795
Let Me Take You by the Hand 9781408713143

Fiction

The Emancipation of B 9781782798
The Silence Diaries 9781789041828
And this shall be my dancing day 9781803412450

Preface

There are some 400,000 Quakers throughout the world, most of them in Africa. For historical reasons, there are different traditions in different parts of the world. Some are more akin to evangelical churches; some are pastor-led. Although all Quakers have much in common, I can only write about my own tradition, the unprogrammed liberal wing that is to be found in Europe, some parts of the US, South Africa, Australia and New Zealand.

And, though there will be references to the events and attitudes of former times and how things have changed, I will also be concentrating on present-day Quakers. There are enough misconceptions about Quakers based on the bonnet-wearers of the past. This is not a book about theology, it is a book about experience: of others and of my own. The experience of seeking and sensing the presence of God, and how it affects how what we do and how we are in the world.

"Quaker" is a nickname given to us by a scornful judge in the seventeenth century – but it's one we are happy to use. The official name for Quakers is the Religious Society of Friends, and we usually call each other "Friend". As the word "Friend" can be ambiguous, I shall generally use the term "Quaker" here, but where the term "Friend" (with a capital "F") appears, that means the same.

Thanks to the many Friends who have shared their experience and knowledge. They include: Brent Bill, Brother Tobias, Ben Pink Dandelion, Geoffrey Durham, Roswitha Jarman, John Peirce, Mark Russ, Annique Seddon, Ginny Wall, Alex Wildwood. All published work has been acknowledged, and permission has been given by all whose words were given to me informally. All errors are my own.

Thanks to The Friend Publications for permission to quote from *Words* by Harvey Gilman, and to Britain Yearly Meeting of the Religious Society of Friends for permission to quote from *Becoming Friends* and *Deepening the Life of the Spirit* by Ginny Wall.

When quotes are from informal written or spoken contributions, I give the names of the contributors. References from published works are given to the books in Further Reading. Where there is more than one book by an author, the reference in the text gives the date.

1

Introduction

This book is an attempt to answer questions such as "What is prayer?" and to explore whether, when and how Quakers might pray. Do we pray together? Do we pray alone?

If you know anything about Quakers, you'll know that the question in the title of this book is a silly one! We try not to generalise. I can't answer for others; I can only speak of my own experience and understanding, and those I have spoken to or whose words I have read.

I am what might be called a universalist Quaker. Given my background, maybe that isn't surprising. I was baptised and confirmed an Anglican. My Russian mother, a non-practising Jew, became an adherent of the Kabbalah, the mystic end of Judaism, in her fifties, and my father converted from Anglicanism to the Catholic church when I was five. Later in life he was much drawn to a monastic way of life, although he was never accepted into an order. His deep exploration and occasional practice of other religions was evidenced by the large folder of cuttings on all faiths that we found on his death. As I found my way to my own faith, I found to my surprise and delight that, despite our different labels, my father, my mother and I were in the same place. And, recently, I found common ground with my brother, now a practising Jew. When he said, "In the section on prayer in the *siddur* the first sentence is 'To pray is to seek to experience God's presence'", I felt the connection. The commonality of faiths at the mystic level has always been apparent to me. It's not particular to Quakers, and has been expressed by writers from many traditions.

I was brought up, as many have been, with a vague idea that prayer was asking a super-human called God to do something.

In church I would obediently repeat the words in front of me. Even in my agnostic phase, when I'd left prescribed words far behind, *in extremis* I would call out silently from the depths, even mutter a few words, asking for help from I knew not what. When I recovered my faith about twenty-five years ago, and came to Quakers, I still found "prayer" a difficult word, and wondered what it might mean. I was not alone. Even monks talk of going through the motions, and the difficulties of keeping mind and voice in harmony. St Paul expressed the fact that we do not know how to pray. Quakers rarely mention the word, although there has been some very rich writing on the subject, much of it gathered in our book, *Quaker Faith & Practice*.

In 2018, partly to explore these difficulties, I created a card game called The Prayer Game. Not something I ever expected to do. Looking for a different way to approach the subject in a workshop I was due to facilitate, and remembering a sheet I'd seen at the Quaker Woodbrooke Centre for an idea called Worship Rummy, I thought this might be an interesting way to approach it. So, one evening, I sat down and wrote 52 words and phrases that might speak to some people of prayer. And in the middle of the night "Here I am" came to me, and I knew I had to include it. I wrote the words on squares of coloured paper; we played it in the workshop; and one of the participants encouraged me to produce it. To my delight and surprise, this simple game seems to open up the subject for many people from different traditions, including faiths other than Christianity, who find it difficult.

The aim of the game is for each player to end up with four cards that speak to them of prayer. At the end of the game, all share their cards and the reasons for their choices, enabling rich conversations on a subject we rarely speak about. Soon after the game's inception, when I sat down to play it with a group of six Quakers, all of them said, "I don't do prayer". Nonetheless, they played it with surprised enjoyment, and found that many of the words in the game – drawn from many traditions – spoke to them.

So, what is prayer? It's a strange subject for Quakers. In a faith tradition that does not have ritual or a liturgical practice, and for whom prayer is usually mental and often personal, it's hard to define (and maybe also to do).

In some religions – Islam, Orthodox Judaism, Roman Catholicism – spiritual practice, communal or personal, is mandatory. Most Christian denominations and many other religions rely on services led by a priest with set prayers for the whole congregation. The authority of tradition; the structure, the power, of the same words spoken over the centuries: all these are central for many people of faith.

There are those, however, who are increasingly uncomfortable saying words which do not come directly from the heart, and perhaps no longer reflect their own beliefs or experience. Indeed, it is the most often cited reason for people coming to Quakers from other traditions.

When I was attending the Methodist Church, I increasingly found myself frustrated by the framework and the words associated with worship. Either they did not express where I was or I would be troubled by the language used. It felt like I was constantly paddling in the shallow end, unable to reach those deeper waters that I instinctively knew were there. So I got out of the pool! (Tania)

Quakers worship in stillness, but anyone may rise and speak out of the silence. The integrity of words coming from the heart, spoken only to reflect direct experience, is an important aspect of Quaker worship.

It is rare for these words – known as spoken ministry – to take the form of a prayer in any traditional sense; rare that what is said is addressed to God, but very occasionally what someone says does end with "Amen". Before we go any further, let's give a thumbnail sketch of a Quaker Meeting for Worship.

2

Quaker Meeting for Worship

Meeting for Worship is the central and most distinctive activity of Quaker life.

However we experience it, it is not about *what* we worship. Whatever the details of our experience and beliefs, Meeting for Worship is where we come together, where differences melt in the stillness. What we all know is that it is unpredictable, that no two meetings will be the same – it depends on those who are present, how they are present, and what is going on in their lives. And on grace. Essentially, it is a communal exercise – a *meeting* – not just an opportunity for a bit of peace and quiet, not solitary meditation. I like to think of the experience as triangular, involving myself, the Divine, and the others in the room. The more we are aware of others, the deeper the worship will be.

A Quaker Meeting for Worship is hard to describe, although it's easy enough to explain the mechanics – such as they are. We sit facing each other, usually in a circle. We meet in equality, with no one taking charge. The meeting begins when the first two people enter the room, and ends when two people who have been previously appointed shake hands. Then all present shake hands with their neighbour. In that hour in between we still ourselves, waiting, listening for guidance, alert for what might come. We are waiting on God, the Spirit, waiting for promptings of love and truth.

In the silence, we may be emptying, opening, focusing on our timeless centre, the core, the ground of our being, creating a space. We may focus on gratitude or call to our attention those who are absent, sick or recently bereaved or deceased. If someone is moved to speak, when they are clear that what is on their heart (rather than on their mind) is for the meeting and not just for them individually, anyone may stand and speak – this is known as spoken ministry. Any ministry that follows will again be out of the silence and from the heart. It is not a discussion.

Those are the bare bones. But how it feels, what happens in that silence, is wonderfully resistant to generalisation. We can't say what the experience of a Meeting for Worship will be. Nor can we say how it has been for another. Each person will experience it differently, although on occasion over the post-meeting tea and coffee, we may agree that the meeting had been profound. But, perhaps unfortunately, it's not something that we generally discuss.

Sometimes we drop easily into worship. Sometimes we just don't tune in. I think many of us imagine that others in the room are in a state of receptive emptiness or contemplative bliss. We all know times when the chatter in our head gets in the way. Even if we feel that nothing is happening in the silence, we have to trust that nothing, that emptiness, and be aware that it has its own quality and potential; that it might give rise to an awareness later, or in someone else. And at some point, the self-consciousness, monkey mind or the shopping list falls away, and we are left in a calm still connectedness. We have different ways of preparing, of emptying, opening ourselves. Reaching a state of receptiveness doesn't seem to be anything we do as individuals – it seems to come from grace or the collective consciousness. We need to let go of trying.

We may arrive grumpy, preoccupied or anxious. At the end of an hour, having put aside those preoccupations for a while, we have reached a different place. There may have been a shift of consciousness, a greater understanding. In some indefinable way, we are changed. We have been re-energised. And because we know from experience that this can happen, we keep coming.

Here, in the silence, you experience a profound sense of oneness within yourself and with others. It is as though you step off the stage and drama of life and into a very different dimension altogether.

This temporary stepping off the stage of the world and into the cool stillness of meeting for worship has a timeless quality all of its own. For it is here that you put aside your identity as a father, teacher, writer... and simply drift without the "oars" of methods or creeds upon an ocean that carries you to the divine within. (Goodchild, 51)

Brother Tobias, once a member of my Quaker meeting, and now a Franciscan friar, described how he discovered Quakers:

I initially found the phrase "Meeting for Worship" an intriguing one, as "worship" suggested to me an onslaught of praise, a noisy clamour actively instigated by the participants. What I instead encountered was a prayerful equity, a shared space of collective generosity. This allowed the still, small voice to enter in. Worship seamlessly blended into prayer and the resultant inner light reflected back at us in a myriad of ways.

It's that sense of connection that has stayed with me after all these years. I lost count of the times that ministry would be shared by a Friend on a subject that had been on my mind at that exact moment. I found a way into that which is greater than self, a path that transcended anxiety and the fear of getting things "wrong". In short, I knew I was upheld. There is a certainty to love and when it hits home, it transforms everything.

And in the Quaker decision-making process, also a Meeting for Worship and often criticised for its slowness, we are allowing space, time, for a more creative outcome. Waiting in the silence.

Meeting for Worship may be the main communal activity of Quakers, but the Quaker Way is not a once-a-week activity, but something that extends to everything we do together. Worship, whether grace before a meal or setting an intention for decision-making meetings, is the root and context of our communal activities. Mostly in silence.

3

Forms of prayer

If you ask a practising Muslim, Jew, or adherents of most denominations of the Christian faith about prayer, you will probably get a pretty clear answer – at least about communal prayer – giving a picture of traditional services with patterns of familiar words. Less so, perhaps, for private prayer, which varies according to the individual and their need. If you ask a Quaker, there is likely to be less certainty and some discomfort. But what we might agree on, or at least acknowledge, are the usual purposes of prayer, which answer needs shared by most of humanity: praise, thanksgiving, gratitude, confession, forgiveness, petition and intercession for others.

Formal prayer will vary according to various factors such as time of day, frequency, duration, place, posture, order and method. It can be vocal or mental, personal or communal. **Active** prayer begins with a human activity, such as visualisation, chanting, images, ritual, symbols or mantras, which then might lead to meditation. **Mental** prayer is inner, wordless. **Vocal** prayer uses words, usually in a form already written and frequently used.

Some Quakers find traditional prayers helpful; find that in settling into the stillness of a Meeting for Worship or in personal prayer, mantras, repetition of a word or phrase, can aid the settling of a busy mind. One writes that "ready-made words sometimes help", calling them "brief pilgrim words to match my footsteps... those paving stones still, like points on a railway line, switch me on to a praying track. In despair, old words can bring steadiness" (Quaker Quest, 38).

Brent says: "There are times that I pick up the Episcopal book of common prayer or the Catholic prayer book or the Psalms and use ancient words of people of faith. To get me out of a spiritual rut."

On the other hand, Rowena says that her objection to vocal prayer is a) that it is nearly always asking for things and b) telling God what God already knows. I tend to agree, and find that her second point is often the barrier to a traditional view of prayer. As Brent says, it might stop us "praying at all, expecting God the all-knowing to read our minds and hearts and be satisfied". But his answer is:

> Yes, if we approach God with honesty and transparency, we acknowledge that God already knows our hearts, souls, dreams, failings, aspirations, minds and intentions. But by putting words to our prayers, we acknowledge to ourselves what we know of hope, fear and challenge. Our words help us reach toward God with the truth of who we are and what we long for. They also encourage, enhance and confirm our willingness to be changed – when we use authentic, truthful words, that is.

But vocal prayer does not have to be something written by others. It can be written anew. Quaker Mark Russ, leading BBC's Daily Service on 22 April 2022, spoke many prayers written specially for the occasion. Or it can even be spontaneous – what someone says in a Quaker Meeting can be considered vocal prayer, even if it doesn't take a traditional form.

Another Quaker expresses something of the power of vocal prayer when spoken from the heart:

> What you're saying comes out
> But it echoes back into your heart
> And that means that your heart
> Catches the echo
> And that means that the heart is

God, and the heart reads the echo.
(Lucy Varma, aged 8)

Communal prayer

Most communal worship is vocal, structured, programmed: "let us pray" the familiar invitation to assembled church congregations, an invitation to focus their minds on God.

James Newman-Shah, an English Muslim, said that his sense of prayer was enhanced after a recent visit to Istanbul,

> Being able to pray alongside hundreds in purpose-built mosques – I truly value communal prayer as I feel truly part of a religious community. We are taught to go shoulder to shoulder so there is no option of being left out, or praying alone.

Quakers are unusual in having a communal worshipping practice that is based on stillness and largely silent. Silence does not play much of a part in most Christian services. Any such period for private prayer rarely lasts more than a minute or so, and may even be accompanied by an organ playing in the background. In modern times, even more than before, people unused to silence find it uncomfortable, thinking that something has gone wrong.

Personal prayer

After prayer, I feel like I have been washed clean. You will find many Muslims make a private prayer after the main prayer and will wipe their faces, like a symbolic cleansing. (James, Muslim)

For many, private prayer, even if it is silent, is also based on prayer that is vocal, written. However, personal, private prayer is where other kinds of prayer, closer, perhaps, to

Quaker practice, emerge. In all denominations and faiths, there is a contemplative tradition, explored more fully in Chapter 6.

Time, place and posture

In Christianity, although church services can take place on different days of the week, it is on Sunday morning that most church services take place, with evensong another regular occurrence on Sundays, and sometimes during the week. For Jews, the holy day is from sundown on Friday to Saturday sundown. In both religions the weekly event reflects the biblical commandment to rest on the seventh day of the week.

Regularity

Although many religions have set times for specific prayers, there is more flexibility than is generally understood. Hindus are encouraged to supplement set prayers with their own.

Jews are asked to pray three times a day: morning, afternoon, and evening. Praying regularly, it is felt, enables a person to get better at building their relationship with God. However, my brother, a practising Jew, said,

> Of course there are set times for prayer and you are supposed to say the *Schema*, the central prayer of Judaism, first thing when you awake in the morning and last thing at night. There are set prayers that are used at appropriate times but there are times when you will just want to pray. In a sense it seems to me that prayer is something you just do.

There is an inner urge, a call, that is beyond explanation.

Muslims have five prayers they are obliged to perform throughout the day, with timings based on the sun. They follow the same pattern so everyone can follow, and set prayers are always recited in Arabic. But they can also pray at any time.

Quakers consider that there is no set time for worship. Even Sunday Meetings for Worship are a convenience for people who might be working during the week. But Meetings are held on other days, at different times of the day. They can be held anywhere, at any time. As Brent Bill writes in his lovely book *Holy Silence*: "As with any faith tradition, it is the intention to worship that makes a time and place holy" (86).

But some agree with the view of the Carmelite nun Ruth Burrows, that "it is hardly likely that we shall enter fully into the sacramental life, receive the transforming action of God, unless we set aside some time exclusively for prayer" (95). Others, stressing the importance of spontaneity, disagree.

As with those of other denominations, many Quakers find a pattern for their prayer time helpful. A quiet contemplative time, maybe with some spiritual reading, first thing in the morning can set the tone for the day, and at the end of the day, a time to reflect is an opportunity for gratitude. That does not prevent prayer at other times: before a meal, for instance, or an "arrow" prayer in spontaneous appeal. Sometimes those are the times when I feel closest to God.

Posture

In Judaism, in Islam, physical positions, gestures and movement are an important form of ritual. In Tibetan Buddhism, full length prostration is an ancient expression of reverence. In most forms of Christianity, the position for prayer is on our knees. Not so for Quakers, although one Quaker mentioned remembering a time, some thirty-five years ago, when it was not unknown for a Friend to go down on their knees. For Quakers generally the position is immaterial. We tend to sit on chairs, eyes open or shut, feet firmly on the floor, hands held loosely in our laps, finding that the most helpful position to aid the inner stillness we are seeking. But no one will mind if a bad back demands that we lie on the floor, or walk around from time to time. Tradition has it that we stand to speak, to give vocal "ministry", but in a small group, or if the person ministering has difficulty standing, it is not a problem if someone remains sitting. The important thing is that we face each other, that we are in a position of equality. In old Meeting Houses, wooden benches face each other in a square; these days we tend to sit in a circle. At the end we shake hands with each other.

In recognition of the lack of physical expression in our worship, many Quakers engage in such practices as yoga, Tai Chi and body prayer. Many Quakers miss the music from different kinds of worship. They generally find it in other parts of their lives, but sometimes someone will sing in Meeting for Worship, occasionally in the form of a hymn – especially that known as the "Quaker hymn", "Dear Lord and Father of Mankind", written by the Quaker John Greenleaf Whittier (although many are uncomfortable with the very male language of his time). The joke "How do Quakers sing hymns? Slowly, because they are checking the next line to see if they believe it" is based on the same reluctance that prevents them speaking prayers written by and seeming to belong to someone else. A matter of integrity. But sometimes music takes over and Quakers will go to carol services (singing words that they might well not believe) or find an opportunity to sing Taizé chants.

Holy Ground

Most religions have specific spaces devoted to religious practice: buildings on what is considered consecrated ground. A core belief for Quakers is that there is no divide between the sacred and the secular, that no place is more holy than another, and that worship can be held anywhere. From the beginning, Quakers have expressed their faith in the simplest of ways, eschewing religious symbolism and ornamentation, such as stained-glass windows, paintings or sculptures. In the early days Quakers stood out against what they called "steeple houses", but as space ran out for worship in their own homes, they began to build Meeting Houses: simple and unadorned buildings, providing a space without distraction from the essential direct relationship with the Divine.

Simplicity is an important aspect of Quaker life. Some years ago, rather to my surprise, I felt called to move to a much smaller place, to create a space with few adornments, fewer visual distractions from writing, from contemplation. I remember my mother coming round to my small flat, soon after I'd moved in. I'd got rid of a lot of my possessions, and had little on the walls, wanting to avoid unnecessary distraction from being in the moment. She looked round at the almost empty walls and said, with sad disapproval, "Oh, you have changed." "Yes, Mum, I have changed."

That said, I do have a little corner of my sitting room with some of the objects that have a spiritual connection: a little wooden carving of the Buddha, a Thai Kuan Yin statue that belonged to my grandfather, some feathers and a seed pod from a Native American reservation, a silver candle holder. And near by, a wooden statue of the Hindu goddess of creativity, Saraswati.

Some people use such a space to practise contemplation, meditation or prayer. A Roman Catholic friend used to have a large house in Canada which had an altar on every floor. Maybe it is unusual for Quakers, who prize the simplicity of worship, but Quaker Mark Russ writes:

I've embraced a lot of "props" that support me in my prayer life. I recently created a little altar in my study, where I have some icons, a candle, prayer books and other paraphernalia. Creating a little beautiful space makes it easier to maintain a discipline of regular private prayer. I feel called to this sort of life but really lack the self-discipline to do it by myself.

As for churches, "steeple houses", most of us will acknowledge that spaces of any religion that have contained and witnessed worship, often over many centuries, have been imbued with an atmosphere of sacredness.

Sacred books and religious artefacts

Most religious denominations have key religious books. Muslims have the Qur'an; Anglicans have not only the Bible but *The Book of Common Prayer*. Quakers will often find nourishment in books of other faiths, but have no book of their own that is considered holy. *Quaker Faith & Practice* in Britain – which exists in many other countries, often with different names – is a guide to Quaker practice and an important collection of Quaker writings from many sources, but is updated every generation and is not considered more sacred than other books. Nor is *Advices &Queries*, a handy little guide to living the Quaker Way.

Visual representation is core in many traditions. For Hindus a picture or statue of a deity is often the focus for personal prayer or *puja*. In Eastern Orthodox Christianity, icons are seen as a gateway to the Divine. Whether for personal contemplation, or as part of the visual fabric of the church, they are generally copies of more ancient paintings: instantly recognisable images representing an ongoing tradition and community.

Prayer beads are a common resource in many religions. The best known is the Rosary, various forms of which have been in use by Christians since the third century, and particularly the one devoted to Mary, used by Roman Catholics. But prayer beads are important too for other religions. The *japa mala* of Hinduism is used to direct and count the recitation of mantras during meditation, the beads representing the cyclic nature of life. In Buddhism they are said to represent humanity's mortal desires. In Islam the rosary is used in an act of prayer and is carried by all classes of Muslims, especially pilgrims, each bead representing one of the "most beautiful names of God".

For many people – even those who are not affiliated to any religion – lighting a candle is an important way to remember someone who has died or who is in need. For peace or for healing. In Islam, Sufis refer to candles as the divine Light; for Christians they symbolise the Light of Christ. A tangible representation of a practice that Quakers call holding someone "in the Light".

In a beautiful and important essay on religion and symbolism, twentieth-century American Quaker Thomas Kelly explores the use of symbols in traditional forms of prayer and explains why Quakers have dispensed with most of them.

> Grounded in... experience of immediacy, Friends have discounted and discredited the symbols in religion... They have been dismissed as shadows because the substance of the Bread of Life is at hand...
>
> Symbols are stationary, unchanging, frozen, while the life of the Spirit which they symbolize is flowing, growing, changing, ever becoming richer...
>
> And one characteristic of all symbols is that they gesture beyond themselves. They step aside, once our attention has been, by them, directed beyond themselves. Their value is instrumental, lying beyond themselves, rather than intrinsic, lying within themselves alone. (1966: 61, 62, 65)

But two kinds of pointing, Kelly says, remain important for Quakers: the use of language and the importance of action; how helping one person also stands for helping all; the individual pointing beyond to all.

4

Kinds or purposes of prayer

When I came to Quakers, there was no question of recapturing the patterns of my childhood. However, since the Quaker Way came out of Christianity, in exploring what prayer is for Quakers today, and for me, I have found it useful to revisit the primary categories recognised by most denominations of the Christian faith. These are: adoration and worship, contrition, petition, intercession, thanksgiving, and praise. In doing so, there's one vital question we need to address.

Who or what are we praying to?

At the centre of any religion is the relationship with something within and beyond, the Divine, Spirit, the God of many names. As Quaker and Anglican priest John Peirce says: "An understanding of prayer relates to our understanding of the nature of the Divine." For many, God is a problematic word, and concept. Traditional images persist of an old bearded man on a cloud, the Divine with a human and almost always male profile. Memories of a judgemental interventionist God haunt many from their childhood or previous religious affiliations.

One writer in Quaker Quest's little booklet *Twelve Quakers and Prayer* makes a good point when he says: "A traditional understanding of prayer sees God as separate from us." If we see ourselves as "of the same substance, the same eternal spiritual essence as God" (13), our understanding of prayer must change to accommodate a less dualistic view of our relationship with the Divine.

Hinduism has a panoply of gods and goddesses, standing for different aspects of the Divine, and all the Abrahamic faiths – Christianity, Judaism and Islam – assume a belief in a divine being. Certainly, in the early days of Quakerism, when all Quakers were Christian, such a belief would have been assumed, and early writings are peppered with the word God.

Communication

A friend who has spent many years among Buddhists around the world emailed me recently:

> I am reminded of a small prayerful story associated with my Christian father.
>
> One day some years ago, my father and I were in communication via email, enjoying bouncing a few messages back and forth... this was in the days before WhatsApp and Twitter.
>
> I remarked that it was good to be able to share a common thought and heart space in real time from the other side of the world via the internet. I was enthusing about the speed of this then new-fangled cyber communication.
>
> My father wrote back one line:
>
> "I find prayer quicker!"

Patricia Loring describes prayer as talking to God, intentional communication. How a relationship with the Divine is expressed and how communication happens varies. Most prayer in the Abrahamic traditions is about talking to God, and there is very little time given to listening. It is unusual for Quakers, but there are some who say that their relationship with God involves talking, even chatting, to God.

Brent Bill feels that an authentic prayer life is one in which prayer is a never-ending conversation with God, saying that

> one doorway to an authentic prayer life is through language. The conversation of prayer, after all, is communication through words, spoken or unspoken. By praying, we clarify

and express our intention with a level of focus that does not often grace the rest of our daily life. (20)

And does God talk to us? There are few who would admit it. We rarely discuss our most mystic, intimate experiences. Early Quakers, like biblical prophets, often spoke of hearing the voice of God telling them to take a certain course of action. Nowadays I think it is a rare occurrence although Brent says he often "hears" the voice of God, indeed, has a conversation:

> Of course, whilst listening in MfW I often respond to that which I heard with words back to the Divine. And whilst laying my issues out for God in prayer, I may hear That Voice which speaks from beyond me and which is Eternal.

And it did in fact once happen to me. I was walking along the road when I heard, or rather felt, a big voice vibrating within me say "Preach". Preach? I wondered. Quakers don't preach. But over the years I have come to realise that, uncomfortable though I am with the word, perhaps what I have been called to since then – the writing, public speaking, teaching – could be called preaching.

But in general Quakers tend to be suspicious of the "showy" guidance that is more characteristic of the charismatic churches. We generally describe our experiences as nudges, prompts, a sense of inner conviction, which may come during Meeting for Worship or, often unprompted, at other times. For Quakers, prayer is primarily about listening.

New Light

The roots of our Quaker society are indeed Christian, but even the earliest Quakers recognised a commonality with other faiths. In 1693 William Penn wrote:

The humble, meek, merciful, just, pious and devout souls are everywhere of one religion; and when death has taken off the mask they will know one another, though the divers liveries they wear here makes them strangers. (*QF&P*, 27.01)

So, an expression which we often use, and one that is richly explored in Alex Wildwood and Timothy Ashworth's book of the same name is that Quakers are "rooted in Christianity and open to new Light". In recent years, as we have become more exposed to other faiths, the "new Light" has become a much broader spectrum. Many Quakers would call themselves Christian (though their definitions might vary); many would not. As we experience a dynamic Spirit in our individual faith journeys, so, as a collective, our sense of community changes. Until forty years or so ago, most Quakers would think of themselves as Christian to some degree; then in the late 1970s there developed a more universalist strand with the formation of the Quaker Universalist Group in the UK, and the Quaker Universalist Fellowship in the US. Now, questions are raised not only about our adherence to Jesus, but to any kind of theism.

Recognising the riches that the practices and understandings of other faiths can bring, Quakers are happy to embrace people who are also Muslims, Buddhists or Jews; from any other major faith, or none. There are a number of attenders at British Quaker meetings who call themselves Quanglicans. A plurality of adherence is not seen as a threat. Many people come to Quakers from other faiths and retain an affectionate loyalty for their former faith home. They are surprised, and relieved, to discover that there is no expectation that in coming to Quakers they have to cut off their connections with their previous affiliation. That openness has always been the case; even in the seventeenth century, as we see from the William Penn quote, above. But it is only in the twentieth century that it became common for that openness to be in the Quaker community itself, with what is called a "universalist" strain becoming more common. More recently, there has been a growth in nontheism, with some Friends believing that God is a human construct. Not all Quakers believe in God. Many more may not be comfortable using the word but have a sense of something beyond, something within and without.

We may not know what, if anything, we are praying *to*. The Quaker way is unusual in not insisting on a belief in God. For Quakers do not have a creed or the need to sign up to any special belief. The main focus is personal experience. There is a strong belief in continuing revelation, which means that the belief of any of us can change. When I first came to Quakers, I found the word God very uncomfortable. Now, along with Spirit, it is my word of choice for something within and beyond. Others may feel more comfortable with words such as Truth, Light or the Universe.

Quaker and Buddhist Peter Jarman writes:

Prayer, unseen communication, is experiential, but does not require, I believe, a supernatural God with whom to communicate. Prayer is dialogue with my inner guide. (9)

When asked about the Quaker way, a common response is that we believe that "there is that of God" within each of us. In talking to people who define themselves as atheists, my tendency is to ask "What is this God that you don't believe in?" The chances are that I don't believe in that version of God either.

***

The Religious Society of Friends – Quakers – emerged from a turbulent time after the English Civil War, when many groups broke away from the established Christian church. Fundamental to this new movement was to strip away what they considered accretions, to return to a simple kind of worship, to revert to the contemplative traditions of the early church, to establish the authority of personal experience. Surprisingly, there is little about prayer in the writings of early Friends. They speak a lot about preaching, but apart from the occasional instruction to pray, there is no description of what is meant.

One of the rare mentions comes in a description of George Fox, from the preface to the original edition of his Journal:

> But above all he excelled in prayer. The inwardness and weight of his spirit, the reverence and solemnity of his address and behaviour, and the fewness and fullness of his words, have often struck even strangers with admiration, as they used to reach others with consolation. The most awful [Full of Awe] reverent frame I ever beheld, I must say, was his in prayer. (William Penn, quoted in Johnson, 2)

I did come across a mention in Mary Penington's journal, written in the 1650s, about her struggle with prayer before she came to Quakers: at one point, having heard the instruction "Pray continually", she wrote:

> I found that I knew not what true prayer was, for what I used for prayer, an ungodly person could use as well as I, which was to read one out of a book; and this could not be the prayer he meant... My mind was deeply exercised about this thing... I flung myself on the bed, and oppressedly cried out, "Lord, what is prayer!" (quoted in Durham, 111)

She then began to write her own prayers.

So, how do Quakers relate to the traditional categories of Christian prayer? Thanksgiving and gratitude come naturally to most Quakers, even if there is little clarity about to what or whom it might be addressed. These feelings may lead naturally to adoration and worship, but many Quakers feel uneasy at notions of bowing down to some kind of superior being. Casper ter Kuile sees adoration differently: feeling that it is "a chance to get beyond introspection, to connect with something beyond". He says "the very same moment when they feel connected to something more than themselves is when they also feel more authentically true to themselves" (54).

Similarly "contrition", which many connect to previous experiences of confession. Ter Kuile says, "it can be enormously refreshing. Finally! A chance to be honest, witnessed by the great beyond, about what's going on and confront the way we want to show up in the world: braver and free" (*ibid.*).

Petition and intercession/supplication

Petition and intercession are the kinds of prayer that cause problems for many Quakers. Praying *for* things, for ourselves (petition) or for others (intercession), praying that our wishes be fulfilled, no longer make sense to many of us. How would I know what to wish for? Who am I to think that I know what is best? Asking for an outcome makes an assumption about my own knowledge, and expresses my need to be in control. Hard as it may be, a difficult situation may be just what is needed for spiritual growth. A friend once told me that she was glad that she had had cancer, and I know that my own painful times have often led to a richer life, far beyond what I might have imagined or expected. If we are able to contemplate suffering in that way, preferably at the time and not just with hindsight, it might help us to consider difficulties as learning opportunities.

The idea of "praying for" someone or something, when we might consider that all is known to God in any case, seems unhelpful. Only "Thy will be done" seems to make any sense – and we may consider that it will, in any case! But there are other ways of considering petitionary or intercessionary prayer.

I think it's fine to ask for things in prayer – and it might be important to vocalise the things that we really want – but I don't think that the purpose of prayer is to receive the things we ask for. I see prayer as a place to be honest with God about our desires, and allow ourselves to be reoriented towards that which is life-giving, so that we want what God wants. (Mark Russ)

Another way of looking at this came in some spoken ministry in my Quaker meeting recently, when there was a call to focus our energy on being *for* rather than *against* things – so to be *for* peace, *for* justice rather than against their opposites. Then another Quaker rose and said that his way of "being for", was to pray for peace for those suffering from war, justice for those unjustly treated, water for those in drought, food for those who are hungry, homes for those who are homeless, food for those who are starving – and then to orient his life towards those prayers: giving money to charity, working in a school for those on low incomes. Those were his ways of being "for".

The former Archbishop of Canterbury was asked by Mark Tully on the BBC:

How do you feel about intercessory prayer? Yours is very much internal prayer, isn't it?
The Archbishop:
There's no huge difference really. A great Church of England writer of the twentieth century writing to a friend said, "I'm going to spend ten minutes just thinking about you and Jesus", and I think that's a brilliant definition of intercessory prayer. You don't send in your list of requests or bombard God with your demands. You just hold the image and sense of a person or situation in the presence of God as if you want to let the one seep into the other. The bringing together of those two realities in your mind and heart is very much how

I find intercession works.

Mark Tully:

So isn't there any element really of saying to God, "Please help this person" or whatever?

The Archbishop:

Well, of course there is because your emotions are involved here, and in particularly intense circumstances of need of course I say sometimes, "God, *please* make a difference to this". Your emotions push you towards saying these kinds of things, and there's no need to be ashamed of that. But the reality is just to let God into the situation to hold it there. That's the bottom line.

(http://rowanwilliams.archbishopofcanterbury.org/articles. php/660/the-archbishop-on-understanding-prayer.html)

A Quaker, who is also an Anglican priest, writes:

> Prayer is not a "get out of jail free" card – more a place where we can contemplate the Divine in silence – bringing with us into that Light those people, situations, causes that are in our hearts and minds... Not a shopping list but a chance to hold those we love in our compassionate awareness. [upholding]. And to set intentions for ourselves.

Quakers often use the phrase "holding in the Light", a practice that is both inward and outward. We pray not *to* God for others but *for* God for them. Prayer is an act of sharing with God, not an attempt to prompt God into action. I've realised that the outward cause is not changed by prayer. We do not pray to affect God but that we ourselves might be changed in the process. As Diana Lampen says: "It is God at work, not we ourselves; we are simply used" (*QF&P*, 2.26).

In an acknowledgement of our weakness, surrender is more to the point. Dag Hammarskjold said: "Your cravings as a human animal do not become a prayer just because it is God whom you ask to attend to them"! (34).

And we need to remember that prayer is always a commitment. We need to recognise the importance of our involvement, the cost to us. We need to take responsibility for our part in what happens, to allow ourselves to be instruments of God's purpose.

Prayer is an act of sharing with God, the Spirit, and not an attempt to prompt God to action. It is a promise that I will do my best, even if what I am able to do seems too insignificant to be worthwhile. When I pray for peace, and that the hearts of those in authority may be changed, it is a promise that I shall do such things as write to those in power, share in vigils, and above all lead my own life, as far as possible, in such a manner as to take away the occasion for strife between individuals and between peoples. When I pray for others who are in need, it is a promise to make my own contribution, perhaps by writing, by visiting, by a gift, by telling someone whom I know could help. When I pray for forgiveness, for strength and courage, I try to open my heart, making it possible for me humbly to receive. ("Anna", 1984, *QF&P*, 2.27)

There is little point in praying to be enabled to overcome some temptation, and then putting oneself in the very position in which the temptation can exert all its fascination. There is little point in praying that the sorrowing may be comforted and the lonely cheered, unless we ourselves set out to bring comfort and cheer to the sad and neglected in our own surroundings. There is little point in praying for our home and for our loved ones, and in going on being as selfish and inconsiderate as we have been. Prayer would be an evil rather than a blessing if it were only a way of getting God to do what we ourselves will not make the effort to do.

God does not do things for us – he enables us to do them for ourselves. (Elisabeth Holmgaard, 1984, *QF&P*, 2.28)

Does prayer work?

If we are not asking for specific outcomes, what do we mean by prayer "working"? How can we tell if prayer has any effect?

My own belief is that outward circumstances are not often (I will not say never) directly altered as a result of prayer. That is to say, God is not always interfering with the working of the natural order. But indirectly by the working of mind upon mind great changes may be wrought. We live and move and have our being in God; we are bound up in the bundle of life in Him, and it is reasonable to believe that prayer may often find its answer, even in outward things, by the reaction of mind upon mind. Prayer is not given us to make life easy for us, or to coddle us, but to make us strong... to make us masters of circumstance and not its slaves. We pray, not to change God's will, but to bring our wills into correspondence with His. (William Littleboy, 1937, *QF&P*, 2.24)

Many people feel that there is a kind of placebo effect: if people know they are being prayed for, there can be a beneficial effect: patients' health can improve. But there is some evidence to show that even when people don't know they are being prayed for, there is often an improvement in patients' health. A Hindu friend talks of the "good vibrations" received by the person you are praying for.

And there may well be a beneficial effect on the person praying.

She says:

Prayer brings a nourishment to the soul. It also gives you inner strength, a grace, gratitude and being a humble human being. A prayer also brings in clear consciousness to the mind. I think praying is a wonderful way of bringing stability to life but you have to have inner faith.

Dutch priest Henri Nouwen writes:

> People we pray for regularly come to receive a very special place in our heart and in the heart of God, and they are helped. Sometimes this happens immediately and sometimes over time. In addition, an inner community begins to grow in us, a community of love that strengthens us on our daily life. (12)

During the traumatic evacuation of Kabul from the Taliban in 2021, a Friend spoke of her colleagues stuck in Afghanistan, and her own feeling of helplessness. "All I can do is pray, and that", she said with an embarrassed laugh, "seems pretty useless".

It's an honest expression of what many of us may feel when it is apparent that prayers are not in any obvious sense answered. And if that is so, could it be that we were only half-hearted in our approach, maybe not altogether sure about what we wanted?

Mark Russ says:

> Some of my most powerful experiences of prayer have been when I've been prayed over, including laying on of hands. (These experiences have been rare, and I can really see the potential for harm in these experiences if the person praying over you prays for the wrong things.)

Spontaneous

I like to think of prayer as a movement of the heart. Even those who do not acknowledge any faith sometimes call out in spontaneous appeal. I sometimes think that that unthinking reaching out is the time when I come closest to God. It's a time when I and my consciousness are out of the way, when I stand naked in my need.

As for many people of any faith (or none), there is a tendency for prayer to be used only in times of trouble: asking for help, or railing against God. Annique, who in her workshops has led a number of sessions on prayer, writes in her notes for an exercise to encourage personal reflection:

A natural human need to find expression for, maybe a place for our overwhelming feeling – joy/pain – may sound clichéd in expression – God help me, praise the lord, praise be to Allah, even a simple thank goodness – uttered silently, whispered, cried out. Also a spontaneous blessing and gratitude.

To whom was that unconsciously chosen spontaneous utterance expressed – to the universe, to a hearing attentive God? but that is what we are seeking to reach for – something beyond ourselves – a grounding within and a connection beyond ourselves, something to hear and attend – to witness – to seek us as directly as we flounder or glory... or simply live from day to day in our ordinary tasks of life.

This spontaneous sense of the spirit working through us can be experienced also in a sudden thrill/spark of humanity and of loving kindness, the beauty of music, where we are drawn into an eternal moment, trill of a bird singing, sudden recognition of our smallness in the face of the universe and time, a quiet sense of deep sadness.

Grace
My own experience is that what we are given arrives in the most unexpected way. God's ways are indeed mysterious:

any "answer" is indirect. When I am going through a tough time, when I am opening myself to God's mercy, surrendered, something beautiful: a meeting, an affirmation, a kindness, which probably has nothing directly to do with my difficulties, appears. The need is there, admitted, and it is answered. An unexpected and glowing gift that surrounds my soul.

And when I open myself to guidance, when I need to know if I am on the right path, in enabling time and space for the Spirit to enter, I might find a completely unexpected way forward. Frequent obstacles and rejections may show us that we are on the wrong path; affirmations may show us that we are on the right one. And, in my experience, such guidance very often comes through other people. A phone call can open up a new and exciting opportunity, which we would never have thought of on our own. And through a series of seeming coincidences – synchronicities – that move can be confirmed. Tapping into connection, relationship, the linking factor in all living beings, that some feel defines God.

5

Spiritual practice

Spiritual practice, both individual and collective, is common to most religions – is seen as a necessary deepening of the spiritual life. Many feel that the contemplative life cannot be maintained without regular formal practice: an exercise of the spirit, as thought is of the mind, or physical movement of the body. Donald Court, writing in 1970, says:

> The essence is regularity and time – time to reach down to the level where I can begin to see myself and my work straight, where that strength we call love can break through my anxiety and teach me how to respond instead of react. (*QF&P*, 20.09)

I must confess that I am not good at maintaining a regular practice. I do try to do some spiritual reading in the early morning, find time to focus on those in need, and practice gratitude, usually before I go to sleep. But in general, I too easily allow other things to distract me. And I realise that stressing the importance of spontaneity can be used almost as an excuse for not creating a rhythm, not building discipline into one's prayer life.

Quakers have adopted many kinds of spiritual practice: blessing (lovingkindness) practice, listening prayer practice, for example; details of some of these are given in the appendix. Some, such as body prayer, conscious breathing (*pranayama*), walking meditation, walking the labyrinth, are physical. Are they all prayer? And what about meditation? Or pilgrimage, retreat? Is taking time out for various lengths of time not just an opportunity for prayer, but prayer in itself?

Unlike many other practices, Experiment with Light has Quaker origins. It was devised in 1996 by Quaker and theologian Rex Ambler following his study of early Friends' writings. A form of guided meditation, it is often practised in contemporary Quaker meetings in specific Light groups, but it can also be undertaken as a solitary discipline, and it is not necessary to be a Quaker to practise it. Many such meditations ask you to empty your mind, but the Experiment with Light script asks to look into your mind: "Ask yourself, what wants my attention now?" More details of the process can be found on the website: https://experiment-with-light.org.uk/about/

One of the distinctive qualities of the Quaker way is the willingness to learn and borrow practices from other religions. Many Quakers meditate on a daily basis. Mark Russ talks of having "a bank of prayers and practices" which he has developed over the years. He says:

I have "seasons" of prayer, where for a number of weeks I'll be with one practice, and then I find I switch to another. So it's a mixture of freedom and the familiar. It's not something new every day.

Quaker and Buddhist Peter Jarman says he prays and meditates, often using familiar prayers from both the Christian and Buddhist traditions.

Margaret has a little book in which she has written her favourite prayers. She says,

I find it helpful to use forms of words either vocal or otherwise as a lead-in to opening myself up to the power of the Spirit ("the good raised up and the evil weakening" as Barclay put it in the seventeenth century), my favourite prayer being the Lord's Prayer which has become for me all things, e.g., I sometimes use it as a centring device in

Meeting for Worship; I sometimes see it as a sort of mantra which sustains me at times of difficulty.

Quakers who have no background in the Bible or Christian hymns or prayers are less likely to be drawn to their use. Such reluctance can also be true of those who have negative memories of being brought up in a particular tradition, and have come to Quakers wanting to find something different.

A Quaker friend said he felt that our attitude to spiritual practice depends on our temperament. He confessed that his spiritual practice was "all over the place". Whenever he settles down to something structured, he remembers, for instance, that the cats need to be fed. "But," he said, "isn't feeding the cats a spiritual practice? Of course it is."

***

Although, as we have seen, some Quakers find forms and modes of prayer from other traditions helpful, their use is generally in addition to what would seem the core of Quaker prayer, to be described in the last two sections of this book: Contemplative Prayer and Life as Prayer.

6

Contemplative prayer

Many people have been drawn to the meditative practices of Eastern religions without realising that something similar is available nearer to home. Beyond the generally accepted forms and types of prayer lies an ancient and wholly different tradition of prayer, which can be found in most major religions of the world – for example, in Judaism, Islam and Bahá'í. Although often viewed with suspicion by the mainstream Church, contemplative or mystical practice is a longstanding part of the life of Christianity, and can be traced through the seventh-century Desert Fathers and Mothers, to the anonymous *Cloud of Unknowing*, and such mystic figures as Julian of Norwich.

Craig Barnett explains that in affirming the primacy of direct experience, early Quakers felt

> that they had rediscovered the core insights of Jesus and the first Christians, which official Church teachings had systematically evaded, ignored or misrepresented since the 1st Century. The Quaker understanding of Christianity emphasises the primacy of inward experience of spiritual reality – the "Inward Christ". Early Friends understood "Christ" as an inward reality, accessible to every person by experience, to guide and empower them to live the kind of life that Jesus lived. Faith in Christ means trusting in this Inward Guide, which enlightens everyone who is willing to open their lives to it. (https://transitionquaker.blogspot.com/2014/01/christian-roots.html)

In rejecting many of the tenets of the mainstream Christian teachings of the time, early Quakers were in fact tapping into a mystic strand of Christianity that, despite being disowned by the official Church, had never disappeared. And, as witnessed to by many writers and exemplified in the monastic life, it is still a major part of Christian practice today. It could be said that contemplative practice is at the root of all Christian prayer.

***

Contemplative prayer is about being present, and getting ourselves out of the way. It is not escapism or daydreaming, but a deepening awareness of our place in the world, our connection with all that is, and the Divine mystery. Being self-aware but not self-conscious. Contemplative practice requires us to pay attention. Particular spiritual practices such as the Quaker waiting in the Light (listening, letting go, opening ourselves), adopting a contemplative gaze (looking as if for the first time), and the *lectio divina* practice of sacred reading – reading slowly from the heart – can be gateways, can awaken us to an awareness of the Presence.

Communion

In one of his daily meditations, Franciscan theologian Ilia Delio writes:

> Prayer is the longing of the human heart for God. It is a yearning and desire for relationship with God, and it is God's attention to our desire: God-in-communion with us... We long for God because we are created by God, and this longing is both the source of our hope in God and the very thing we resist. (https://cac.org/daily-meditations/opening-to-god-2022-02-18/)

Rowan Williams also feels that, "Prayer is *communion*, it's that allowing the depth *within* and the depth *outside* to come together."

Relationship with all that is

At the heart of contemplative prayer is recognition of our relationship with God, and with each other and all living things as an expression of the Divine. If, as writers from different religions claim –

"Every creature is a word of God" (Meister Eckhart, medieval Christian mystic).

"The universe is a constant prayer" (Vivekananda, Hindu).

"Everything that is being itself is a prayer" (Franciscan priest, Richard Rohr) – then every response from us is a communication.

I asked the earth, I asked the sea and the deeps, among the living animals, the things that creep. I asked the winds that blow, I asked the heavens, the sun, the moon, the stars, and to all things that stand at the doors of my flesh... My question was the gaze I turned to them. Their answer was their beauty. (St Augustine, quoted in O'Donohue, 22)

Prayer is attuning yourself to the life of the world, to love, the force that moves the sun and the moon and the stars. (Steindl-Rast, xvii)

I sat in a prayerful way in quiet seclusion, walked in the beautiful natural landscape, played with my family, laughed with friends at myself and at our communal joy and felt that deep sense of connection, the sense of oneness with all things – the deep sadness or joy feels to me like a sense of connection beyond ourselves – a oneness – the emotion becomes something more... A sense of Presence. (Annique)

The Jewish prayer is very connected with the nature and the history, in a way of blessing. You pray according to the moon, the time in the day. You pray according to season, blessing the beginning of the flowers of fruit trees, blessing the good smell of a flower, blessing God when you see rainbow... (Therese)

Prayer brings a nourishment to the soul, a connection, a hope, and praying for every being also brings peace to the soul. (Harsha, Hindu)

Attention and intention

For a long time, I had a problem with the idea of prayer. The turning point, the moment when the word began to have some meaning for me, came when I heard the definition of prayer as "attention". As the French mystic Simone Weil wrote: "Prayer... is the orientation of all the attention of which the soul is capable towards God" (66). The power of focused positive thought or feeling. And that focus, that attention, is key to my understanding.

Like the Quaker Meeting for Worship, contemplative prayer is a waiting upon God; it's about listening, not talking. Seen this way, prayer becomes a spacious place in which to listen, to receive, to align ourselves with God's will. It includes adoration, wonder and contemplation. Being in loving relationship.

Wherever there is love, there is only prayer. When our heart is in the right place and brimming with love, everything becomes prayer. (Steindl-Rast, 78)

It is an experience of surrender. Silently, in stillness. Not word-based, either mentally or aloud. Sometimes in desperation it will be a more active asking to be shown the way. But not asking for outcomes. How can we know what they should be?

I try to make this way of being a part of all I do all the time. I am not always successful, but my need for worship in my private life seems to have come as an extension of Meeting for Worship: the need for silence extends into the rest of life.

It is also intentional, an act of faith and will. Patricia Loring calls intentionality our ultimate concern, part of the unification of the divided self, and defines it as "the relationship of attraction between ourselves and that which draws us" (48).

> Turning to the Spirit, even for a moment, takes us to a deeper place of connection. I believe this is reaching deep within ourselves for the strength to face what it means to be human in this world – to steady ourselves – a reaching beneath conscious thought – a desire to give attention to [we know not what or whom], to focus. To mark peak experience. A moment between breaths, a regular practice of meditative prayer, a regular reading, a pause between one activity and the next, to uphold someone. (Annique)

Prayer is to prepare ourselves, to open ourselves to God's will, and make ourselves channels for God's love, the Spirit. It is a passive state, and many testify to the feeling of not so much praying as being prayed through.

Centering prayer

A more recent development in Christianity is that of centering prayer, a practice that its founders claim has its roots in the contemplative prayer of the Desert Fathers of early Christian monasticism, and in works like *The Cloud of Unknowing* and the writings of St Teresa of Ávila and St John of the Cross.

The name was taken from Thomas Merton's description of contemplative prayer as prayer that is "centered entirely on the presence of God". In his book *Contemplative Prayer*, Merton writes "Monastic prayer begins not so much with 'considerations' as with a 'return to the heart,' finding one's deepest center, awakening the profound depths of our being in the presence of God" (5–6). Many Quakers would relate to that.

Ginny Wall writes:

Centering Prayer is rooted in the Christian contemplative tradition. At the heart of the practice is the act of surrender to the loving power of the divine. It is a practice not of attention or concentration but of "letting go and letting God". The prayer consists of an inner gesture of release, making space for the Spirit in our hearts. The intention to be open to the work of divine love within is the key to Centering Prayer. A simple word, or the breath, is used as an anchor for our intention, but it is not a mantra to repeat or concentrate on; we simply return to it each time we realise that we have become distracted by a thought or sensation, as a way of re-focusing. (2012: 15)

***

So, what, for Quakers, is prayer? As we can see, there is no clear definition. It is not a word that is often used. Even early Quakers, who were all Christian, hardly mentioned it. The UK version of our little guide to the Quaker Way, *Advices & Queries*, mentions prayer a number of times, but doesn't really say what it means.

We are urged to pray for one another (number 18) and less specifically "Seek God's guidance" (25 and 27), "Bring" things or people "into God's light" (32). Numbers 10 and 35 refer to "prayerful support". Number 13 asks us to "Pray that your ministry may arise from deep experience, and trust that words will be given to you", and number 29 to "pray that in your final years you may be enabled to find new ways of receiving and reflecting God's love".

An earlier version, quoted in *Quaker Faith & Practice* 2.20, is more emphatic:

Do you make a place in your daily life for reading, meditation, and waiting upon God in prayer, that you may know more of the presence and guidance of the Holy Spirit? Do you remember the need to pray for others, holding them in the presence of God? (*Queries*, 1964)

So Quaker *Advices and Queries* seems to take it for granted that we do pray. No 10 says that "prayer, springing from a deep place in the heart, may bring healing and unity as nothing else can". This is in the context of the advice to "let meeting for worship nourish your whole life". There seems little differentiation between prayer and worship, which is the word most often used by Quakers.

So far, we have mostly been exploring personal prayer, whether we pray alone. But, to go back to one of our original questions: Do we pray together?

Worship/prayer

As we discussed at the beginning, Quakers rarely say a traditional prayer during our collective Meeting for Worship. So, do we pray collectively at all? God, worship and prayer are all words which carry baggage for many, and have to be unpicked in a delicate and personal way.

If worship is being in the presence, listening, opening, waiting, the same could be said of prayer. Maybe for Quakers there is little distinction between them: the two often seem to be used almost interchangeably. Indeed, in much of Quaker writing about prayer the word "worship" could be substituted.

So, what for Quakers is the difference? Is prayer something done in the context of worship? One of the problems with this question is that Quakers use the word "worship" both to mean our Meeting for Worship and more broadly, as when someone leading a session may say "let's have some worship" in the way that a Christian minister may say "Let us pray".

I asked a number of Quakers about the difference, and, typically, they gave a variety of responses. So, to look first specifically at Meeting for Worship:

I think the difference between Meeting for Worship and prayer (though they can blend) is that in Meeting for Worship I go with the intention of listening. In prayer, I go with the intent to lay my concerns in the lap of our loving God. Not that I do either of these well, but that's how I see the difference between the two. (Brent)

In Meeting for Worship I feel that we are opening ourselves to communication with God and each other through prayer. (Margaret)

In centering prayer one pays attention and hopes for nothing and in Meeting for Worship one listens and hopes for an encounter. (Stuart Masters)

We have seen that traditional forms of vocal prayer are rarely used in Meeting for Worship, but in a broader definition of worship, can there be said to be a difference between prayer and worship? Geoffrey thinks perhaps not: "the word may be synonymous with prayer for many of us". But he goes on to say:

My sense is that the two words overlap, but are by no means interchangeable.

The word "worship" is used by Quakers as if we all know what it means. I'm quite clear that I don't, and that, by using it as we do, we confuse more people than we help. If I had to give a quick definition, I might say that it's a mixture of prayer, adoration, upholding, learning and, very occasionally, religious ecstasy. And gloriously, it is never the same twice.

Similar words could be used in a similar way to describe prayer, but that doesn't make them the same thing. Quaker worship can be aided – or interrupted – by a person offering spoken words.

In other words the silence and the speech can be catalysts for sudden insights or a total loss of concentration. Prayer is usually a more private matter.

Other comments included:

It does seem to me that worship and prayer are closely linked and often overlap, but certainly in the more pastoral traditions prayer is seen as a distinct spiritual practice. One that grows out of worship, to be sure. (Brent)

I think prayer and worship are very close together, especially as encounters are profound but usually fleeting but prayer can continue around and form part of worship. (Nuala)

Worship may include prayer but prayer is also in its own category. (Ben)

Worship is when I arrive. Prayer is what I do to get there. (Annique)

Of course, no one can say that prayer is easy. We are reluctant to stop, make room for the Spirit to enter, to "waste time with God". Busyness is so much easier. Quakers are bidden to come to Meeting for Worship with hearts and minds prepared, but too often we rush from other activities, and rarely arrive having settled ourselves into a receptive state. Finding a time, a place of solitude in silence, may create conditions that are conducive to prayer but, just as in Meeting for Worship, thoughts of the to-do list may intrude, so in solitude other thoughts may distract. In either case, even with no words to hide behind, it is easy to fool ourselves. It is important not to get discouraged, but to persevere. As Thomas Merton, a Trappist priest who knew a thing or two about solitude and prayer, says, with our backs against the wall, "we pray to pray".

And while these special conditions may help, they are not necessary. In the natural world, or when faced with a beautiful piece of art or music, prayer, gratitude, may just come upon us unbidden.

When describing the Quaker Way, we frequently refer to the fact that we don't generally define ourselves by belief, that we are reliant not so much on authority as on our own experience. We say that ours is an experience-based religion. So, what kind of experience are we referring to? I presume it is a direct relationship with God, the mystic connection which we feel is accessible to everyone. So, is that prayer?

7

Life as prayer

Contemplative life is a human response to the fundamental fact that the central things in life, although spiritually perceptible, remain invisible in large measure and can very easily be overlooked by the inattentive, busy, distracted person that each of us can so readily become. The contemplative looks not so much around things but through them, into their center. (Nouwen 1995, 36)

If prayer is not defined by tradition, form or specific practices, what is it?

If prayer can be at any time, in any place, if there is no distinction between the sacred and the secular, might we say that prayer is more a state of mind and heart than an action? A place. A place of contemplation. Living, being in that state.

Acknowledgement of our weaknesses (contrition), forgiveness – yes, these are traditional forms of prayer that would resonate with the needs of most of us. And, yes, Quakers may find a specific focus for their attention: a few moments of silent thankfulness before a meal, gratitude at the end of a day – but in general, prayer is less about specific subjects than about a way of being that is all-encompassing. Not a divided life in which there are times for prayer and times for other activities, but a way of life that is embedded in prayer, in which all stems from, is rooted in, prayer.

Most of all, I realise that in attempting to be open to guidance in all that I do and am, prayer – my relationship with the Divine – is central to my life. To live our faith is to try to live constantly in the presence of God, to keep that awareness in all that we do, in contemplation of the Presence within and without. A constant receiving and giving. Like contemplation, this way of life is embedded in many religions. Brother Lawrence, a seventeenth-century French lay brother, wrote a slim little volume of letters and essays called *The Practice of the Presence of God*, describing his life in just such a way: doing everything, every small thing, for the love of God.

A monk once told me that "prayer is not so much a matter of words or ideas but rather a deep, inarticulate longing for one in whom one's whole being can rest and be at peace". We all have our individual relationship with prayer, our own practice, our own understanding of what it means. In the end, it is important (in the words of Dom John Campman) to "pray as you can, not as you can't".

American priest Barbara Brown Taylor, writes:

Prayer... is waking up to the presence of God no matter where I am or what I am doing. When I am fully alert to whatever or whoever is right in front of me; when I am electrically aware of the tremendous gift of being alive; when I am able to give myself wholly to the moment I am in, then I am in prayer. Prayer is happening, and it is not necessarily something that I am doing. God is happening, and I am lucky enough to know that I am in The Midst. (From *An Altar in the World*, quoted in https://www.aamboli.com/quotes/book/an-altar-in-the-world-a-geography-of-faith/4)

And many Quakers also affirm the centrality of prayer in their lives.

One's prayer life – in word, in seeing, in movement, in action, in silence – is an expression of that unique incarnation of the divine which each of us is... Prayer is the voice of life itself speaking through our particular being. Finding the right manner of prayer for oneself is a form of self-knowledge. (Gilman, 22)

I began to realise that prayer was not a formality, or an obligation, it was a *place* which was there all the time and always available. (Elfrida Vipont Foulds, 1983. *QF&P*, 2.21)

A Quaker prayer life arises from a life of continuing daily attentiveness... a practice of patient waiting in silence. (Johnson, 1)

Service

In an online "Enquiry into Prayer" hosted by Woodbrooke in May 2022, ten Quakers were asked to choose from a list three words that most spoke to us of prayer. One of the words, which I did not choose, but which has stayed with me, seems quite different. That is the word "service". That it is our service, our action for others, that represents prayer. As Mother Teresa wrote: "Prayer in action is love. Love in action is service." And Henri Nouwen:

To pray means to open your hands before God... Praying is not simply some necessary compartment in the daily schedule of a Christian or a source of support in a time of need, nor is it restricted to Sunday mornings or mealtimes. Praying is living. It is eating and drinking, acting and resting, teaching and learning, playing and working. Praying pervades every aspect of our lives. It is the unceasing recognition that God is wherever we are, always inviting us to come closer and to celebrate the divine gift of being alive.

In the end, a life of prayer is a life with open hands – a life where we need not be ashamed of our weaknesses but realize that it is more perfect for us to be led by the Other than to try to hold everything in our own hands. (https://henrinouwen. org/meditations/open-yourself-to-god/)

At one stage of his ministry as a priest, John Peirce was asked to lead social responsibility work with the churches in Devon. He says:

> I don't know that I believe in *labore est orare* (to work is to pray) but we were trying to show that prayer should lead into and arise from practical action. I was also learning that through our efforts God can be seen to act in the world.

The American Quaker Thomas Kelly, writes of "simultaneity": of living our lives on two levels at once.

> On one level we may be thinking, discussing, seeing, calculating, meeting all the demands of external affairs. But deep within, behind the scenes, at a profounder level, we may also be in prayer and adoration, song and worship and a gentle receptiveness to divine breathings. (1941: 35)

Practice

As we saw in Chapter 5, with details in the Appendix, there are many helpful specific practices: prayers, maybe, in themselves. But in considering life as prayer, practice needs to be more deeply embedded.

Practice can be such a small matter: a pause for gratitude before a meal; indeed, a pause before embarking on any activity, to make its intentionality clear; a pause during the day to take stock, centre ourselves. Even in the busiest of times, we can pause, perhaps when we are travelling to work or going upstairs. I love the phrase: "Between actions, pause and remember who you are." In that pause, like the moment between one out-breath and the breathing in, or between a wave receding and the swell of the next, is a space of another dimension. During mental prayer or meditation, just the act of gently brushing away random thoughts is a spiritual one, a declaration of priority and intention.

In order to try to stay in that place, I find it important to have some consciously more withdrawn periods of contemplation. For me that is generally early in the morning and last thing at night, with attempts to collect myself at odd moments during the day. Less noise, less intake of information: allowing the silence of worship to spill into the rest of my life. With opportunities for online worship increasing, I find that tuning in several times a week helps me to maintain or recover a peaceful heart. Enabling a more spacious consciousness for grace to enter in. As the French monk and sannyasi Abhishiktananda says: "God dwells only where man steps back to give him room."

How important it is to clear a space in our lives to be still, listen, give the inner voice a chance. To remove ourselves from the and then and then of our lives, what John O'Donohue calls "the pedestrian sequence of time". To retreat, pause, have awareness in our doing.

> When I am not present to myself, then I am only aware of that… mode of my being that turns outward to created beings. And then it is possible for me to lose myself among them. Then I no longer feel the deep secret pull of the gravitation of love that draws my inward self toward God. My will and intelligence lose their command of the other faculties. My senses, my imagination, my emotions, scatter to pursue their various quarries all over the face of the earth. Recollection brings them home. It brings the outward self into line with the inward spirit, and makes my whole being answer the deep pull of love that reaches down into the mystery of God. (Merton, 1955: 195)

Brent Bill refers to the apostle Paul's invitation to "pray without ceasing":

Then surely everything is prayer. That's something I resonate with. I once heard prayer described as passionate thinking and I do a lot of that. Things I care deeply about are always in my mind and heart and so perhaps I am praying without ceasing as the apostle Paul put it. I think it is sort of the Quaker version of praying the hours done by liturgical Christians. Instead of set times with set words, we're doing it from the heart in every moment.

Brother Tobias, whom I first met many years ago when he was a member of my Quaker Meeting, makes the same reference. He talks of having become a Franciscan,

> paradoxically embracing the liturgy and sacraments that seemed so bewildering at the time... But Quaker prayer remains with me in the sense that as a Franciscan I am called to "pray without ceasing", to embrace the Spirit that nurtures and sustains us. That gentle openness underpins my calling and ministry, and it was originally shown to me by the Society of Friends. I will always be grateful.

As so often, the Quaker Thomas Kelly is inspirational:

> How, then, shall we lay hold of that Life and Power, and live the life of prayer without ceasing? By quiet, persistent practice in turning all our being, day and night, in prayer and inward worship and surrender, towards Him who calls in the deeps of our souls. Mental habits of inward orientation must be established. An inner, secret turning to God can be made fairly steady, after weeks and months and years of practice and lapses and failures and returns. It is as simple an art as Brother Lawrence found it, but it may be long before we achieve any steadiness in the process. Begin now, as you read these words, as you sit in your chair, to offer

your whole selves, utterly and in joyful abandon, in quiet, glad surrender to Him who is within. In secret ejaculations of praise, turn in humble wonder to the Light, faint though it may be. Keep contact with the outer world of sense and meanings. Here is no discipline in absent-mindedness. Walk and talk and work and laugh with your friends. But behind the scenes keep up the life of simple prayer and inward worship. Keep it up throughout the day. Let inward prayer be your last act before you fall asleep and the first act when you awake. And in time you will find, as did Brother Lawrence, that "those who have the gale of the Holy Spirit go forward even in sleep". (Thomas R Kelly, 1941, *QF&P*, 2.22)

8

Some Quakers now

In the enquiry into prayer, mentioned earlier, the similarities in the words chosen were striking. Many chose "waiting" and "grace"; most choices drew on experiences of the passivity of prayer, a sense of being prayed through. And in choosing a question for us all to consider, it was a sense of mystery that drew us: in the process, the outcome and the nature of any possible recipient.

This book has been enriched – no, largely formed – by what Quakers have spoken and written about prayer. I want to end with a few contemporary voices expressing some of the ineffability of this subject.

Roswitha Jarman

I have no final answer to what prayer is, but here are my thoughts:

I have four ways of praying,

One is a daily stillness (with occasional lapses) which holds in the light family and friends. It is not asking for anything, but it simply holds "in the light".

A second is deep prayer as I understand it, a third is comfort prayer and the fourth is life as prayer.

True prayer for me is submission.

Submission to

the stillness to the spirit, to the mystery.

To emptiness, *my just being*.

To standing (sitting/lying) in awe.

To acceptance of what is.

To knowing myself not in time, but in eternity.

To knowing myself not as a separate self, but as interbeing with all.

And in a real deep moment even "myself" is washed away.

Comfort prayer I need at times for my own comfort; it has words and images.

It is the child longing for the comfort of the parent.

This comfort prayer can express itself in sheer agony and frustration.

As well as in joy and thankfulness.

But even this comfort prayer is directed to the unnamed presence.

Fourthly, I have times when life is prayer.

All I do and experience is prayer.

Unceasing prayer.

Ginny Wall

My take on prayer is that it's a word that alludes to a state or practice that brings us closer to an experiential knowing of our true nature, which is the Divine Self, the Oneness from which we spring, and which we finally come to know we never left.

The different "types" of prayer are simply different expressions of or gateways into that knowing, that Presence. They suit different personalities and needs, but most importantly different stages on the path "home" to remembering our Divine nature. So, for example, supplication, verbal prayer and intercession may be more suited to us when we see ourselves as separate small beings coming into relation with a Divine "Other". More contemplative forms of prayer may well suit us as we come closer to an intuition of our Oneness with the Divine, where words no longer serve so well to point to that which is beyond words. But this is not exclusive, as different personalities may still engage with practices that seem not to fit so well the overall stage they are at, but are actually very effectively meeting needs at a level of their being that still benefits from that form, eg., a contemplative monastic whose main practice is silent contemplation, but who enjoys the rhythms of liturgy and certain verbal prayers.

Meditation can operate at all levels of consciousness, from practices that aid with stress and pain management through to meditations that draw us deep into wordless, expansive Awareness.

Meeting for Worship can straddle these worlds too, in my experience. Where there is much verbal ministry, especially where it comes from the shallower levels of consciousness, it may work to keep some folk more in the human mind/ego level of consciousness, while still tuning us very gradually towards sinking deeper into Being. At the same time, individuals in a meeting like this may nonetheless go deep in the Silence. And certainly, whole meetings can go deep together where silence is given space, and spoken ministry is drawn from those deeps.

Indeed, everything can become prayer. This is a response to the call deep within us to realise our true, Divine nature, and unfolds as an experience of life where gateways to Presence are sought and seen everywhere.

Harvey Gillman

Prayer... is... recognition of the limitation of the self, an intentional turning of the self to the Light, of the part to the whole, the individual to the community and to God. It is the very encounter of the energy of the self with the energy of creation. Perhaps it is out of this that miracles may occur, And who knows, it may be out of this that prayers are answered (22).

Janet Scott

Prayer: Where we are meant to be; what we are meant to do; and how to find the strength to do it.

Pierre Lacout

Prayer is... a secret between God and the soul (36).

Tania Brosnan

I have come to believe prayer to be the still point deep within. The place where the Divine and I become one. This sacred presence is always there and so informs who I am and what I do. Sitting in the silent worship of the Quaker faith, I immerse myself in its depth and wait for the still small voice, a voice that does not only speak to me but reaches out to the community with whom I am silently worshipping. I like to believe all the still, sacred depths in the room gather to create a well of Divine influence.

So prayer is not something I do, prayer is something carried within me. It is what and who I am... Divine love in action. I try to pause from time to time and intentionally remind myself of this sacred presence that is prayer and allow it to shape who I am.

I still love words, but far more is said and heard in the silence.

Like others, Mark Russ's definition encompasses different approaches:

> I think prayer is mysterious, and is about being with mystery. At the same time, I find there's a real power in naming and vocalising. For me, prayer is about survival, keeping going, a regular returning to the Spirit for strength.

As for me, when playing the prayer game, perhaps the four prayer cards I would choose today are: "Attention", "Intention", "Living in the Presence" and "Love".

Oh, and "Here I Am". That'll do.

As you can see, Quakers have a complicated relationship with prayer. When I mentioned the title of the book, some of the responses I got were: "Let me know when you find out!", "Some do, some don't", and "It all depends what you mean..."

But, to try to answer the question, Quakers may not use the word "prayer", may not relate to traditional kinds of prayer but, when viewed in the context of the rich possibilities encountered in this book, then, yes, yes, I think we do.

Appendix: Some spiritual practices

Body prayer

Gather ourselves in: Stand with bare feet comfortably apart and hands out. Feel the floor or grass beneath your feet, your grounded connection to the earth. Slowly bring your hands together, gathering all that you are, all that is loveable, wonderful, joyous, as well as failures and shortcomings, bringing together all the parts that create your individual unique whole.

Focus. Bring your hands together, palm to palm at heart level. This signifies our intent to be present to God, our desire to offer consent to God to move within us.

Offering up all that we are. Arms reaching up, hands open in petition, reaching out to express our longing and yearning to God.

Receive. Lower hands, palms up, to receive what God has to give us this day: gifts, counsel, comfort, joy, awakening.

Taking what is given into ourselves. Cross hands over chest, taking the God-given gifts into ourselves, feeling them throughout our whole body, absorbing them into our being.

Offering God's self, God's gifts to the world. Lower arms, palms facing forward to express our sharing of God's gifts with others: loving service and ministry flowing through us (adapted from Deborah Shaw, *Being Fully Present to God.* South-Eastern Quaker Yearly Meeting, 2005).

Review of the day

The Jesuit practice of Examen has been taken up as a useful practice by many outside the Catholic church. It can be a form of looking back over the past twenty-four hours, keeping an awareness of the presence of God in our lives. Reflecting on the events of each day can help us see the work of the Spirit in our lives – the sacred in the everyday. Like beachcombing, this practice can help us notice all kinds of things which we may have passed over in the busyness of the day. As you prayerfully explore the mystery of yourself in the midst of your daily actions, you can grow more familiar with your own spirit and become more aware of the promptings of Love and Truth within you. Begin by taking a moment to still yourself and become open to the presence of God/Spirit (Wall, 2010: 269).

Loring (36) gives us a simple form it might take:

Where have I met and co-operated with the Spirit today?
Where have I met and evaded the Spirit today?
How do I speak to God about this?

Or

Where was Love today?
How did I miss it? Meet it?

The following practices are from *Becoming Friends* by Ginny Wall.

A blessing (lovingkindness) practice

In the Christian tradition blessing practices involve asking that God's love enfold or protect someone, while in Eastern traditions "lovingkindness" towards the self and others is practised to bring a deep realisation of oneness with all beings.

1. Begin by taking a moment to still yourself and become open to the presence of God/Spirit.
2. Bring a person to mind whom you wish to bless, or evoke lovingkindness for. This can be someone you love, someone you hardly know (for instance, someone you met in a shop this morning) or someone you find difficult.

You can also practise blessing yourself – sometimes this can be the most important place to start.

3. Now spend some time in silence simply upholding that person, "holding them in the Light" (to use the Quaker expression).

4. You may then like to use some very simple phrases to focus your upholding of that person; these can be repeated silently or under your breath throughout your period of prayer. Phrases could include one or two like the following:

may you be well
may you be free from suffering
may you be happy
may you be at peace

bless you in your sleeping
bless you in your waking
bless you in your work
bless you in your play
bless you in your good moods
bless you in your bad moods
bless you when you....

It can be very healing to use a blessing practice towards someone with whom we have argued or have a difficult relationship, or again towards ourselves, choosing relevant phrases such as "bless you when you stay out all night".

5. Bring the blessing practice to a close by spending a short time in silence, allowing the Light of God's love to shine on you and anyone whom you have been upholding (2010: 266).

A simple breathing practice

Practising mindful awareness of our breath can be a helpful way to become centred at the beginning of meeting for worship and can offer, in its simplicity, a profound experience of connecting with the sacred in the present moment.

1. Begin by taking a moment to check your posture. You can, of course, do breathing practice in any position, but it can be very helpful to sit in a well-supported upright position: whatever position you choose, the important thing is to find one that enables you to be both relaxed and alert.
2. You may find it helpful to close your eyes gently.
3. Take a moment to release any tightness from your muscles – you can do this by imagining tension simply flowing away on each outbreath for several breaths. Don't forget areas that are often quite tense, such as shoulders, back and face.
4. Now bring your focus to your breathing. Simply let your attention rest on your breath, allowing it to flow naturally. Follow your breath with your full attention as it flows in and out of your body.
5. As you watch, notice how each breath is different: sometimes shallow, sometimes deep; smooth or ragged; fast or slow; cool or warm; silent or with a sound.
6. You may like to focus your awareness in one place as you watch your breath: the rise and fall of your chest or abdomen, or the feeling of air passing at the back of your throat or through your nose.
7. Continue to watch your breath with mindful attention for the rest of the time you have set aside.
8. Each time distractions arise, just bring your attention back to your breath, gently and without judgement. There's no success or failure. Just breathing. Simply being present to what is (2010: 275).

A contemplative prayer practice

Contemplative prayer involves any practice through which we seek to be aware of the presence of God/Love and to remain silently and attentively in that presence, completely open to God. Prayerfully repeating a single word or short phrase is one form of contemplative prayer, designed to help us swim out beyond the ego and realise our oneness with the Divine. As we pray, our will keeps consenting to God by returning to the sacred word. This simple but demanding discipline helps reduce the obstacles to an expanded awareness of a fuller level of reality.

1. Begin by finding a quiet place where you can sit in a well supported position.
2. Close your eyes lightly.
3. Sit relaxed but alert. Take time to become quiet and centred. You may find that gently focusing on your breath helps.
4. Silently, within your own heart, begin to say a single word or short phrase. You may consider one of the following or choose your own:
   Peace
   One...
   Love
   Jesus...
5. If a word does not come immediately, allow yourself to wait on a word and trust that it will come. This may take several prayer sessions, but this waiting in itself is a practice of surrender. You can use your breath as a focus until a word comes.
6. Listen to your prayer word or phrase as you say it gently but continuously. Allow the repetition to be an anchor for your intention to be open to God's presence.

7. Do not try to think or imagine anything – spiritual or otherwise. When thoughts or other distractions come, do not try to suppress them but just keep returning gently to your word or breath (2010: 267).

Sacred reading practice (*lectio divina*)

Sacred reading has been part of the Christian prayer tradition for centuries and is an important spiritual practice for many modern people. It is different from our normal, analytical reading of information and involves a slow meditative reading of a short text – reading not so much with the mind as with the heart.

1. Begin by choosing a short extract from a sacred text: this could be the Bible, poetry, other sacred writings or anything that speaks deeply to you. Even this choosing can be done in a way that allows the text to "choose" you, rather than you making an intellectual selection; for example, you could choose at random from a collection of extracts or use a lectionary or book of daily readings.

2. Read the text slowly and meditatively two or three times. Allow the words to soak in.

3. Is there a word or phrase that jumps out at you? Allow yourself to become aware of any words that cause a particular response, whether because they speak deeply and positively to you or perhaps cause resistance in you.

• Now read the passage again, lingering over this word or phrase. Pay attention to what resonates in you, to your own response to the words. Stay with the word or phrase and repeat or reread them as often as you wish. It can be helpful to spend 10 or 15 minutes simply meditating on the word or phrase by repeating it (aloud or silently) in this way.

4. Allow the words to speak to you at a deep level. What is the Spirit teaching you through this word or phrase and your response to it?

5. If you feel drawn to make any kind of response to this deep reflection, give expression to it: this could be in prayer, writing, drawing, or simply speaking to God about it.

6. Then spend some time in silent waiting on God – not necessarily expecting an answer to any questions, but simply resting in contemplation of the Divine presence in your heart.

7. As you move back into the ordinary activities of your day, do you feel called to live out any understanding you have reached as a result of this practice of sacred reading? (2010: 270).

Some Questions

Some questions that you might find useful personally or in group discussion.

What would you define as prayer?

How do you pray?

Why is prayer important to you?

How often do you pray?

When did you start praying?

Is there a difference between when you pray alone and when in Meeting?

Do you use prayer aids, including Quaker ones?

How important is silence in your prayers?

How does being a Quaker affect the way you pray?

If you use the Bible, why and how do you use it to help you pray? Could you give some examples?

Further Reading

Quaker Faith & Practice (QF&P). 5th edition. London: The Yearly Meeting of the Religious Society of Friends (Quakers), 2013

Ashcroft, Timothy, and Wildwood, Alex, *Rooted in Christianity and Open to New Light*. London: Pronoun Press, 2009

Bill, Brent J., *Holy Silence*. Grand Rapids, MI: Eerdmans, 2016

and Jennie Isbell, *Finding God in the Verbs: Crafting a fresh language of prayer*. IVP USA, 2015

Burrows, Ruth, *Living in Mystery*. Lanham MD: Sheed & Ward, 1996

Durham, Geoffrey, *The Spirit of the Quakers*. New Haven and London: Yale University Press, 2010

Gilman, Harvey, *Words*. London: The Friend Publications, 2016

Goodchild, Christopher, *Unclouded by Longing*. London: Jessica Kingsley, 2017

Hammarskjöld, Dag, trans. W.H. Auden and Leif Sjöberg, *Markings*. London: Faber, 1966

Jarman, Peter, *Seen and Unseen – Ways of Being along Quaker and Buddhist Paths*. London: The Kindlers, 2018

Kelly, Thomas, *A Testament of Devotion*. New York: Harper & Bros, 1941

— *The Eternal Promise*. New York: Harper & Row, 1966

Johnson, David, *A Quaker Prayer Life*. San Francisco: Inner Light Books, 2013

Lacout, Pierre, trans. from the French by John Kay, *God Is Silence*. London: Quaker Home Service, 1985

Loring, Patricia, *Listening Spirituality, vol. 1: personal spiritual practices among Friends*. Washington DC: Openings Press, 1997

Merton, Thomas, *No Man Is an Island*. Tunbridge Wells, Kent: Burns & Oates, 1955

—*Contemplative Prayer*. New York: Crown Publishing Group, 2009

Nouwen, Henri, *Discernment*. London: SPCK, 2013

—*The Genesee Diary*. London: Darton, Longman & Todd, 1995

O'Donohue, John, *Divine Beauty*. London: Bantam Press, 2004

Quaker Quest, *Twelve Quakers and Prayer*. London: Quaker Quest Network, 2015

Steindl-Rast, David, *The Music of Silence*. Berkeley, Ca: Seastone, 1998

ter Kuile, Casper, *The Power of Ritual*. London: William Collins, 2020

Wall, Ginny, *Becoming Friends*. London: Quaker Books, 2010

—*Deepening the Life of the Spirit*. London: Quaker Books, 2012

Weil, Simone, trans. from the French by Emma Craufurd. *Waiting on God*. London, Fontana, 1959

CHRISTIAN ALTERNATIVE
BOOKS

THE NEW OPEN SPACES

Throughout the two thousand years of Christian tradition
there have been, and still are, groups and individuals that
exist in the margins and upon the edge of faith. But in
Christianity's contrapuntal history it has often been these
outcasts and pioneers that have forged contemporary
orthodoxy out of former radicalism as belief evolves to engage
with and encompass the ever-changing social and scientific
realities. Real faith lies not in the comfortable certainties of
the Orthodox, but somewhere in a half-glimpsed hinterland
on the dirt track to Emmaus, where the Death of God meets
the Resurrection, where the supernatural Christ meets the
historical Jesus, and where the revolution liberates both the
oppressed and the oppressors.

Welcome to Christian Alternative... a space at the edge where
the light shines through.
If you have enjoyed this book, why not tell other readers by
posting a review on your preferred book site.

Recent bestsellers from Christian Alternative are:

Bread Not Stones
The Autobiography of An Eventful
Life Una Kroll
The spiritual autobiography of a truly remarkable woman
and a history of the struggle for ordination in the Church of
England.
Paperback: 978-1-78279-804-0 ebook: 978-1-78279-805-7

The Quaker Way
A Rediscovery
Rex Ambler
Although fairly well known, Quakerism is not well
understood. The purpose of this book is to explain how
Quakerism works as a spiritual practice.
Paperback: 978-1-78099-657-8 ebook: 978-1-78099-658-5

Blue Sky God
The Evolution of Science and Christianity
Don MacGregor
Quantum consciousness, morphic fields and blue-sky thinking
about God and Jesus the Christ.
Paperback: 978-1-84694-937-1 ebook: 978-1-84694-938-8

Celtic Wheel of the Year
Tess Ward
An original and inspiring selection of prayers combining
Christian and Celtic Pagan traditions, and interweaving their
calendars into a single pattern of prayer for every morning and
night of the year.
Paperback: 978-1-90504-795-6

Christian Atheist
Belonging without Believing
Brian Mountford
Christian Atheists don't believe in God but miss him:
especially the transcendent beauty of his music, language,
ethics, and community.
Paperback: 978-1-84694-439-0 ebook: 978-1-84694-929-6

Compassion Or Apocalypse?
A Comprehensible Guide to the Thoughts of René Girard
James Warren
How René Girard changes the way we think about God and
the Bible, and its relevance for our apocalypse-threatened
world.
Paperback: 978-1-78279-073-0 ebook: 978-1-78279-072-3

Diary Of A Gay Priest
The Tightrope Walker
Rev. Dr. Malcolm Johnson
Full of anecdotes and amusing stories, but the Church is still a
dangerous place for a gay priest.
Paperback: 978-1-78279-002-0 ebook: 978-1-78099-999-9

Readers of ebooks can buy or view any of these bestsellers by
clicking on the live link in the title. Most titles are published
in paperback and as an ebook. Paperbacks are available in
traditional bookshops. Both print and ebook formats are
available online.

Find more titles and sign up to our readers' newsletter at
http://www.johnhuntpublishing.com/christianity Follow us on
Facebook at https://www.facebook.com/ChristianAlternative

Also in this series

Quaker Quicks - Practical Mystics
Quaker Faith in Action
Jennifer Kavanagh
ISBN: 978-1-78904-279-5

Quaker Quicks - Hearing the Light
The core of Quaker theology
Rhiannon Grant
ISBN: 978-1-78904-504-8

Quaker Quicks - In STEP with Quaker Testimony
Simplicity, Truth, Equality and Peace - inspired by Margaret Fell's writings
Joanna Godfrey Wood
ISBN: 978-1-78904-577-2

Quaker Quicks - Telling the Truth About God
Quaker approaches to theology
Rhiannon Grant
ISBN: 978-1-78904-081-4

Quaker Quicks - Money and Soul
Quaker Faith and Practice and the Economy
Pamela Haines
ISBN: 978-1-78904-089-0

Quaker Quicks - Hope and Witness in Dangerous Times
Lessons from the Quakers On Blending Faith, Daily Life, and Activism
J. Brent Bill
ISBN: 978-1-78904-619-9

Quaker Quicks - In Search of Stillness
Using a simple meditation to find inner peace
Joanna Godfrey Wood
ISBN: 978-1-78904-707-3